SHRINK RAP

PUNH
on the Analyst's Couch

Edited by Peter Barnes

A PUNCH BOOK

Published in association with

GRAFTON BOOKS

A Division of the Collins Publishing Group

LONDON GLASGOW
TORONTO SYDNEY AUCKLAND

D0234548

Grafton Books
A Division of the Collins Publishing Group
8 Grafton Street, London W1X 3LA

Published by Grafton Books 1986

Introduction and selection © Punch Publications Limited 1986

British Library Cataloguing in Publication Data

Shrink rap: 'Punch' on the analyst's couch.
1. Psychoanalysis – Caricatures and cartoons
I. Barnes, Peter
741.5'942   NC1763.P78

ISBN 0-246-13063-6

Printed in Great Britain by
William Collins Sons & Co Ltd, Glasgow

All rights reserved. No part of this publication may be reproduced, stored in a retrieval system, or transmitted, in any form or by any means, electronic, mechanical, photocopying, recording or otherwise, without the prior permission of the publisher.

Introduction

If you meet someone at a party who claims to be an advertising salesman or a bank manager but who seems to know little or nothing about the subject, there's a fair chance that he or she is a psychiatrist or a psychologist attempting to travel incognito. Several psychiatrists and psychologists of my acquaintance adopt this ruse in an effort to avoid the two questions that they dread most when the layperson learns of their profession. These are, in order of appearance, "Oh dear, does that mean you can tell what I'm really thinking?" and "Tell me, what *is* the difference between a psychiatrist and a psychologist?"

Punch cartoonists, it would appear, have progressed beyond these elementary questions and have well-worked-out ideas of the range of the psychiatrist's competence and of the apparently more mundane life of the psychologist (invariably spent in the company of the white rat). The future of the *chaise-longue* manufacturing industry seems secure if they continue to be employed in the super-abundance indicated on the following pages. Equally secure is the future of the shrinks themselves if the range of problems depicted here is a true reflection of the real world. Not for nothing has the scenario of the psychiatrist's couch regularly attained a high place in the league table of popular cartoon clichés over the last two decades.

I suspect that cartoonists would profess no particular difficulty in identifying the coy party-going psychiatrist. They seem to operate with a small number of visual stereotypes, each bearing some resemblance to Sigmund Freud himself. Baldness, a beard and glasses are high on the list of requirements, with a bow tie appearing often enough to be noteworthy. So, when Noel Ford wants to illustrate the problems of a patient unable to delegate, we recognise at once that it is the psychiatrist lying on the couch and the patient taking notes. And Birkett needs no caption at all to make us laugh at the African witch-doctor psychiatrist wearing the Freud lookalike mask.

In these days of sexual equality it is notable that all the cartoon psychiatrists are male. The defensive artist may insist, with some justification, that this is only indicative of the balance within the profession. But the give-away is that 99 per cent of the patients are male as well, which ain't so in real life. Do we need to be trained psychiatrists to recognise that these male cartoonists are merely projecting themselves through their art? Rorschach, thou shouldst be living at this hour!

But not all psychiatric problems are manifested from a supine position. What people say to each other in their living-rooms, or in the pub or in the street is all grist to the psychiatric mill and for these scenes to be amusing assumes a public awareness of conditions such as paranoia, depression and neurosis born of at least some personal experience. It's a shared experience that *Punch* cartoonists have made much of.

The universal experience of having been a child, if not of having children of one's own, adds poignancy to the cluster of cartoons depicting parental concerns for the proper development of their offspring. The knowledge that so much of this effort is doomed to failure is merely underlined by Mike Williams's Child Guidance expert bargaining with his son over the phone in an attempt to get him to pass on a message. If the psychologist can't do it, what hope the mere mortal parent?

Nor, according to the cartoonist, does the hapless psychologist fare much better when experimenting with animals. Pavlov must have had his time cut out mopping saliva off the floor, and most of the laboratory rats know their way round the maze of life far better than their white-coated mentors. There is little doubt that in the party portrayed by Banx, the rats are enjoying their work so much that they can even admit to their occupation!

Peter Barnes
April 1986

"*Furthermore, I am not talking to myself. I am talking to you.*"

*"And I'm supposed to take this seriously?
Having my psyche examined in
the street!"*

"Do you mind? I happen to be next."

"Tell me, how long have you had these hallucinations?"

"I don't suppose it's much compared with other inferiority complexes."

"OK, you blew the first day. But today is the second day of the rest of your life."

"That's it! . . . That's it! . . . Now when you're really gloomy try dipping it in treacle!"

"I've been wearing my husband's clothing again, doctor."

"*Your sexual desires are so odd that I suggest you start demonstrating for your rights immediately.*"

"We're not going to get anywhere unless you make your mind up – either you're a repressed gay or you're a tea-pot."

"Trust people! Trust people! You sound like my other psychiatrist."

"Still, I suppose you psychiatrists hear this sort of stuff all the time."

birkett

"Because it's there."

BANX

BANX

"Bed wetting? You didn't tell me about the bed wetting!"

"There's always one."

"As long as there's nothing wrong with me, I'll be getting back to Jupiter."

"And how long have you been convinced you're a telephone box?"

*"How long have you had this fear of heights,
Mr. Winthrop?"*

"I keep thinking people can tell I'm wearing a toupée, doctor."

"Doctor – I'm happy, why?"

*"It all started when the bottom fell out of
the chaise longue market."*

"I'm not getting thirty to the gallon!"

"It's our dominant father."

"In my opinion he's got an unfortunate manner."

"My last psychiatrist had to have an intestinal by-pass."

MAHOOD

"Tell me. Dr Eichhorn, if I marry Alex, will I become part of the
solution or part of the problem?"

"You'll never solve your problems by
jogging away from them."

"Frankly, Mr Wallace, unless you're prepared to make a serious effort you're going to be stuck with your inability to delegate."

"Can't go on. All I have in life is gone. Stormy weather. Since my man and I ain't together. Keeps raining all the time."

"When did you first start hearing a moo moo here and a moo moo there, Mr. McDonald?"

"You're not the psychiatrist your father was."

"I'm half inclined to diagnose
schizophrenia . . ."

*"I thought I had better ask for a **third** opinion – the **second** psychiatrist said Freud was as mad as I am!"*

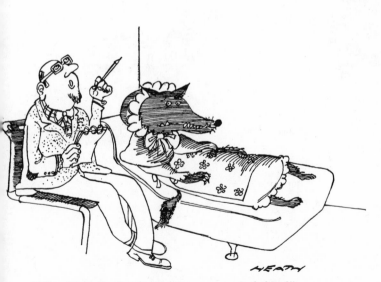

"When did you first feel the need to wear women's clothing?"

"Basically you're not bad.
It's just that everybody expects you
to be bad, and that makes you bad."

BANX

"Do I ever feel depressed?
What kind of a question
is that? I'm a lemming."

"You really need something to take your mind off your hobby."

"There's nothing I can do for you – you are a duck."

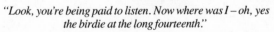

*"Look, you're being paid to listen. Now where was I – oh, yes
the birdie at the long fourteenth."*

"Where shall I leave the horse?"

*"He's a megalomaniac with a marked inferiority complex –
thinks he's Napoleon III."*

"This is going to be a tough one – he thinks he's Napoleon in drag."

"I've been wearing my wife's clothing again, Doctor."

"My knowledge of history is somewhat sketchy."

"Not much of a psychiatric unit, though, is it?"

*"Thank you Doctor.
You do wonders for
my fits of
depression."*

"His methods are unorthodox but he does get results."

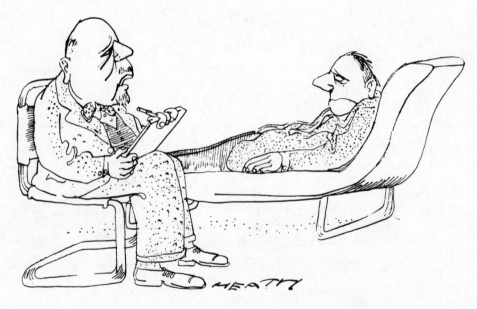

"Oh, don't take any notice of me, I'm just a little depressed."

"*Your 50 minutes are up, Mr Orshatzky.*"

"I've told you before – we're going to get nowhere until you learn to leave your shoes parallel to each other and at right angles to the skirting board."

"He's a well-known psychiatrist who believes that mental illness should be encouraged. This has made him a contemporary cult hero."

"Now there's a coincidence, Mrs Bixby – I had an extraordinary dream about you last night as well!"

"I thought I'd made it clear I was never to be disturbed during regression."

"*I have an alternative psychiatrist – he slaps you around and tells you to pull yourself together.*"

*"Come on, Wentworth – you psychiatry students don't actually **need** one."*

"I see he's solved the problem – he used to worry about always dreaming he was doing that."

"Not to worry, madam. This is a recurring
dream in which I always wake up when
we reach Cockfosters."

"It says – 'Please call a psychiatrist; I am only
trying to draw attention to myself'."

"I'd say loosen his flies but who listens to sex therapists?"

"Well congratulations, Mr Harvey, your fears concerning how much all this is going to cost you are perfectly rational."

"*Well, Miss Fanshaw, I've been seeing you privately every week for ten years now, and my summing-up of your problem would be that you have more money than sense.*"

"*Sure you're dependent on me for psychotherapy. But it's reciprocal.
I need your money to finance my son's sex change operation.*"

"Yes, what is it? I'm very busy . . . ."

"I'm off next week to the World Psychiatric Conference, so you'll just
have to bottle everything up till I get back."

"Are you sure that nobody's following you? We have a special discount on paranoia this week."

"They're all jealous, of course, because I conquered my paranoia."

"Since you ask, I feel that this gentleman's paranoia is the more realistic of the two."

"I used to feel paranoid until I realised there are those in positions of power who <u>want</u> us to feel paranoid."

*"You know what I wish? I wish I were paranoid – then at least I would **think** people were noticing me."*

"You were perfectly all right until you started to let your depression get you down."

'Golly, I'm glad you noticed! There's no point in suffering from depression if nobody notices.'

"Enid, why can't we get depressed as a family?"

"I'm fed up taking the anti-depressants."

"You have lovely teeth. You should take anti-depressants more often."

"I just have the feeling that this anxiety attack is going to be a really bad one."

"He has this thing about walking on cracks in the pavement."

"I've been invited to a Valium morning."

"Just because I don't make a great fuss about my inhibitions doesn't mean I'm not inhibited."

"I went on an ego trip once and nobody noticed."

"So then she called me an egoist and went home to my mother-in-law."

"*Apparently, my delusions of grandeur knock everyone else's into a cocked hat.*"

*"I don't know what I would have done
without Freudian therapy – Sam
transferred all his aggression towards me
to his analyst and is now doing ten years
for assault!"*

"Of course, it's all thanks to my psychiatrist really – if he hadn't sent me on holiday, I'd never have met you . . ."

DREDGE

"Megalomaniacs Anonymous? – it's me!"

Hawker

"I've decided not to continue with aversion therapy."

"That's his shrink."

"Now, you take Spiro. You'd never catch him going to a psychiatrist."

"Are you expecting a case of agoraphobia?"

"*And you owe thirty seven pounds fifty on this one.*"

"Well, it looks as if you're on your own again, Mr Brindley."

"Yes, the usual order – two dozen custard pies."

GROUP THERAPY
ROOM

"I did it! I did it! I traumatised the whole group!"

HUMAN
RELATIONSHIPS
CONSCIOUSNESS
TRAINING
INSTITUTE
UNLIMITED

MON - FRI
11:30AM - 4PM

"I can feel! I can feel!"

"*Do you, therapy group A, take thee, therapy group B, to relate to and empathise with through trauma and depression . . .*"

"At a party, Irwin, why do you insist on labelling everyone?"

"*I often think that it would be nice to have enough self-confidence to project my shyness as an endearing quality.*"

"*Boy oh boy! Is he repressed!*"

*"I feel frightfully inadequate. Don't seem to have any
pent-up frustrations or anger to release."*

"So all right, big shot; if you were tackling a subject like 'Identity Crisis,' how would you picture it?"

"There can't be many people who get into Mensa through the back door, Mr Phipps."

*"Oh, Gerald – you haven't failed the
entrance test for Mensa again?"*

"I wonder how long it will be before we can start testing its IQ?"

"He's quite remarkably average for his age."

"The O'Briens' kid was having screaming fits by that age."

"Nine years old and he doesn't even know how to manipulate his parents."

"The Educational Psychologist says he has a viewing age of twelve."

"On the other hand, he has a disrupting age of 18.2."

"*As a child psychologist of twenty years' experience, my considered opinion is that two rounds with Henry Cooper would do him the world of good.*"

"My! When I last called, your pile of child care magazines was only that high."

"Hurry! I'm helpless! He's eaten the index and three chapters of my Doctor Spock."

*"Oh, by the way . . . according to my teacher I'm suffering from a lack
of discipline in the home. See to it, will you . . . ?"*

"*Hello, Dr. Spock. Say, I hate to bother you, but I've got this forty-year-old kid.*"

"That's what comes of neglecting to ask his teacher to tell him to obey his parents."

*"Oh, be as late as you like . . . but remember,
every minute past midnight hastens us along the treacherous
road to teenage delinquency."*

"If it was discipline you needed, why didn't you ask for it?"

"*Look at it like this, Father – if they're going to rebel against their upbringing, why not bring them up the wrong way?*"

"You do that again and I'll have you child-guided!"

"Look, Timothy, if I give you the two bars of chocolate and the ten new pence, will you tell Mummy that Daddy's on the telephone?"

"I won't pay the fine! I won't, I won't, I won't!"

"I've never been a great believer in all that child psychology stuff . . ."

"That's the best I can do. If you'd like to see another Child Psychologist . . ."

DicKinson

"George! What are you doing with the baby?"

Gahan Wilson

"Yes?"

"Don't you think you're slightly overdoing your experiments on that poor dog?"

*"We might have something
here on aggression control."*

"Good news, Professor Fishbane – we got the rat grant."

"Frankly, Henshaw, if gates go on falling like this, I can't see us ever finishing our paper on crowd hooliganism."

"If you ask me, he really abuses the system."

BANX

"Now this is what I call psychological reseach."

BANX

BATCH
9/C 10/X

"...while those rats receiving B-12 showed quite remarkable initiative..."

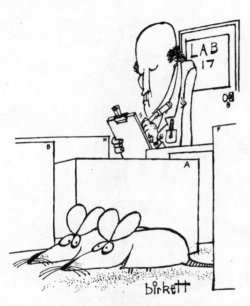

*"I'm getting him conditioned beautifully
– every time I run through the maze, he
throws me a bit of cheese."*

*"But, son! If you don't study, hustle, work, how can
you ever hope to get to the end of the maze? . . ."*

"That's life. What you gain on the food pellets you lose
on the electric shocks."

"See how we've trained them always to pick up the right card when we give them an electric shock."

"This dummy hasn't even twigged how to use a maze."

"We're going to have to split those two up."

"It's certainly going to give the psychologists something to think about, anyway."

"Ignore him, he's just the caretaker."

"He's been falsifying research data for years."

"*I'm worried – he chose that bloody
awful wallpaper himself.*"

"*Well done, Haskett – the research grant is yours.*"